Starving For Leadership: Unconventional Warfare, Special Forces and Startups

E.M. Burlingame - 蒲奕言

ISBN:
ISBN-13: 978-1-7928-0048-1

DEDICATION

For my daughter Hailey. Greatest leadership responsibility I will ever be so blessed with. May you live in a world and future with real leaders and true leadership. May you, in your time, in your own right and way, be a leader.

CONTENTS

ACKNOWLEDGMENTS

In this life so far, I've been blessed to have known and receive guidance, supports and painful confidence building lessons from more than a few incredible individuals. For which I'm immensely and eternally grateful. Even if some of those blessings, supports and guidance were not so comfortably received.

1 INTRODUCTION

"When I was coming up as an entrepreneur, I had to fight for everything I got, and there was no clear roadmap of how to be successful."

– Jason Calacanis – Angel Investor

Brooding, Oxford educated, brilliant 29-year-old, oft maligned as liar, charlatan and fake, you're a maverick Army Officer. You've uniquely adapted to your environment and enemy, more importantly, your partner force, masters of desert power, the Arabs. Traditionally, encounters between East and West are difficult, British officers preferring discipline, order, structure and routine, war with big armies, massive firepower in pitched battles, main forces crushed in a single blow. You develop a different way, dressing and living like the locals, adopting their customs, their ways of thinking. You go native. And it works. It works because you, trained archeologist with previous experience in Syria, know the material you're working with, understand the Eastern way of war. Tentative, hit and run, a reducing of the enemy through a thousand small cuts over protracted periods. Instead of seeking to turn your allies into soldiers, as ordered, you adapt their wisdom, wisdom of the desert. Namely, reality must be accepted as is or you die. Westerners impose reality through brute force and denial, Easterners accept reality and use it. You develop a method of war accepts what is, now, and it works, works incredibly well. Your way is to win hearts and minds, dig into the population, building an unassailable base while remaining decentralized, operating in small groups, striking only where element of surprise can be maintained. Cut them again and again till they bleed out.

You're Thomas Edward Lawrence (1888 – 1935). It's WWI. You'll develop a revolutionary military theory, drawing upon ancient practices modernized in the Boer Wars, theories will survive and act as basis of guerrilla warfare to this day, more than a hundred years later. Ireland 1921, China 1949, Cuba 1959, Rhodesia 1979, Mao, Giap and Che, insurgencies and insurgent leaders all relied heavily on your theories. You were first to understand the new center of gravity is not the battlefield, it's the human domain, the populace. You recognized through lenses of military and rebel theorist, the power of small, well organized, trained, prepared and properly motivated teams of local peoples. You understood modern warfare is population-centric, where victory arises from harnessing intangibles while leading.

***

At some point in life, whether through choice or simply following natural flow of career or life progression, at times having it forced upon, some of us decide to develop ourselves into skilled managers, to take that extra responsibility for our organization, community, for others. This mostly because the need for management expanded dramatically during the industrial era and has become ever more in demand in the postindustrial era. Eras of ever more refined job titles, roles and responsibilities. Eras of increasingly narrowly defined and trained specialists requiring management. Over the course of the past two and a half centuries, the need for quality managers and the role of management have expanded at an exponential rate. To the point now, where professional managers are pumped out of graduate schools and corporate training and private certification programs at ever increasing rates around the world.

In this same two and a half centuries, the Age of Management, we've lost something, something absolutely critical to the long-term future of humanity. We've lost what it means to be an "Leader". In this age we've increasingly conflated skilled management with leadership. Conflated A-Types and their bluster and force and the passive-aggressive and their disruption wither leadership. This conflating, giving real leaders and real leadership negative images, greatly degrading influence and importance. We've gotten to point where we no longer recognize real leaders or leadership, outside the extraordinary. Worse, we've lost most understanding and knowledge as to how to work with leaders to develop their leadership. More critical and dangerous still, we've lost how to develop our own leadership, develop ourselves into real leaders.

This is not to say great leaders have not risen here and there, some despite, often in conflict with, the trend. Gandhi, Aung Sun Suu Kyi, Martin Luther King, Nelson Mandela, Einstein, Welch, Musk, Mohammad Ali and others. To name only a few of those recognized. This is also not to say great leaders are not out there even today and in great numbers, though for the most part, we don't know their names, nor do we recognize their leadership contributions. At a time when the global economy and thereby all humanity, is going through a massive and dramatic change on scope and scale with that of the industrial revolution and thousands of years before, the agricultural revolution. At a time when all of humanity around the world is becoming interconnected and interdependent, as human civilization is changing at a pace never before imagined. We need leaders and true leadership, Influence-based Leadership. Now more than ever, we need strong leaders, not A-Types now associated as. Despite this, in our greatest time of need, vast majority of leaders around the world, true leaders, choose to remain quiet, unobtrusive, relatively unrecognized, so they may, unmolested, continue their work of influencing those around them, leading their community or subset of to improved conditions, better futures, even if only marginally better.

While this "Quiet Professionalism" is to be applauded, when looking to invest in or when assembling and developing a founding team for a startup, we look for Influence-based Leadership above all other considerations. Individuals with a vision for the future, constantly improving their knowledge, removing inherent biases and filters such they see and accept all the many obstacles will be in the way of attaining that vision in the real world. Not simply charismatic, driven or forceful individuals seeking to be the boss, nor those seeking to be recognized as a highly successful manager. Not to detract from importance of all. Instead, we look for those few with real spark of leadership, actual Leaders. Individuals out there putting in that hard effort, always at their own expense and on their own time, developing their own style of leadership, diligently seeking to become foremost authority in their market, or even better, across markets and in the broader community.

When seeking out these leaders, we don't know and don't need to know what leadership is exactly, simply to recognize and develop it when we see it. We don't need to know if leadership is inherent at birth, something developed over time or immediately in response to extraordinary need. Will leave answer to these, more difficult questions for the psychologists, neurologists, geneticists and all the many others rapidly improving our understanding of the human brain and mind, helping us answer definitively nature vs nurture or nature and nurture. We do need be able to recognize signs of leadership within ourselves and others. More importantly, we need know how to improve our own and other's ability to lead.

In what so far has been a completely unexpected and unpredictable thirty-year career, I've had great fortune to work in many different capacities and domains, at many different levels, in most corners of the earth. During this time, I've been truly blessed to meet and work with incredible individuals from every walk of life, to participate in identifying, teaching, training, investing in and developing leaders from small to great. And in these thirty years, my thoughts as to what leadership is, the importance of leadership and how to develop leadership and leaders, has changed many times, sometimes dramatically, at times quite painfully.

We're living an age where leaders are needed perhaps more than any other time in history. Particularly, startup and startup investment leaders. Not only in Silicon Valley and its analogs, but in every community. Those creating new wealth, new industries and knowledge economy jobs. That is, as globalization increasingly integrates and automates, moving us steadily into a post-labour world. A world we are not yet ready for. In times like these, where absolutely everything is changing, and the rate of change is accelerating. We need rebel leaders, in the vein of my childhood hero, T.E. Lawrence. This book shares lessons I've learned at the confluence of Special Forces and technology startups, of how we identify and develop these leaders and their leadership. Whether self of others.

2 ACTIVE INVESTING

"...you should make a contribution...least 10 times what is already out there. A hundred times would be even better. But if you don't strive for a 10-to-one improvement, you won't be successful...That's so fundamental a rule that it tends to be forgotten. There must be high risk — in fact, very high risk. It's the key to success. If there is no risk, you have already missed the boat. Your competitors will already be there."

– Thomas Perkins – Father of Venture Capital

Formerly general and governor of Kahlu, you assume the throne of Assyria in a coup d'état during civil war, killing the royal family, setting Assyria on path to a revitalized empire. In your time you will conquer or subjugate most all the world and peoples then known to Assyria and go on to be recognized as one of the most successful military leaders in world history. While your military leadership was impressive, it's your reforms will revive Assyrian hegemony in the Near East and set pattern for all rulers after you. In the years of your rule (745–727 BCE) you introduce sweeping changes to government, introducing formal civil, military and political systems. You instituted policies to reduce the power of officials, who previously attained immense power, destabilizing the empire and causing great harm to her people. And you create the world's first professional standing army, comprised not only of Assyrians but also of the peoples from all corners of your empire, a professionally trained and equipped army, capable of protecting the empire year-round. You are, Tiglath Pileser III and your leadership and achievements ensured you created the greatest political and military entity of the era, the model future empires are based upon.

***

Over course of last forty-years, virtually all new industries, vast majority of new wealth, and greater portion of new jobs, have come from advances in technology brought to market by startups. More than a few of which are today the world's most influential corporations. All made possible through advent of venture investing and efforts of active venture investors. Mostly centered here in Silicon Valley. Efforts led by pioneers, like Thomas Perkins of Kleiner Perkins fame and others. Much like Tiglath-Pileser III, who in the 8th century BCE established the new model and paradigm for governance we still follow today. The model and paradigm for the new global economy has been well-established and proven. At heart of this new economic model are startups and startup investing. So why are so few attempts to replicate this model around the world meeting with success, despite massive investments in Capital, resources and management? Of greater concern, why is it, current failure rates in venture backed investing even here in Silicon Valley, now average around 75%?

There's no lack startups to invest in, with more than 500,000 launched each month. Nor is there shortage of Capital, as there's an estimated $1.8 Trillion and rising in Capital committed to private equity with nowhere to invest. Nor is the issue insufficient innovation, with R&D spending surpassing $2 Trillion in 2017. These are staggering numbers only rising as incubators, accelerators, competitions and other entrepreneur programs spring up globally. Imagine impact to local, national, regional and the global economy, of wealth and job creation, particularly in developing "pre-emerging markets", if even ten percent of investors shifted focus from playing the numbers game, to seeking out, investing in and developing leaders, quality leaders.

This isn't happening, instead we're doubling down on the now global numbers game and relegating developing markets to modern philanthropy known as "impact investing". As with Shalmaneser V, Tiglath-Pileser III's son and successor, it's a matter of leadership. Here in Silicon Valley and in her analogues globally, Market forces ensure at least a third of failed startups could never succeed, remainder fail due to insufficient leadership. Leadership within the startup most certainly. More critically, lack of active investing leadership from early-stage venture investors. At a time when we should be substantially increasing investing in early-stage knowledge economy startups around the world to ensure more manageable transition into a post-labour global economic system, the opposite is happening. This, despite massive effort and commitment to foster the very thing. Instead there's been a marked decline in early-stage venture investing over past two years. This is coupled with fact, in many parts of the world, particularly developing markets, despite heavy investments in entrepreneur and startup programs, there's no local early-stage investors outside impact investors, who rarely if ever, invest in the kind of securitized assets required in the modern economy. And who simply can't invest at all in many of the communities require it the most. Even in many emerging markets there are very few to no real early-stage knowledge economy venture investors, investing in securitized "for stock" companies. Experts argue there's more than one reason this Angel and Seed investing is slowing down or failing to emerge.

In order of frequency argued these are:

1- Lack of sufficient exit opportunities, as stated;

2- Cyclical nature of the investment industry as whole;

3- Powerful technology corporations with ever larger cash reserves;

4- Growing number of global startup incubators, accelerators and competitions; And

5- High rate investments at this stage return $0 to investors and shareholders.

Taken individually and collectively, all are very valid reasons for decline in early-stage investing over past two years, and for failure of early-stage investing communities to arise in emerging and developing markets. Engaging with Seed/Angel investors, VC and PE friends and colleagues past two years, all incredibly busy making and managing investments, consensus is, there's a real shortage of quality startup and early investor leadership, leaving little option but to continue the numbers game. This is particularly troubling, as at this place in larger investment cycle, more often than not, and increasingly as financial market dynamics evolve, exit is through acquisition.

Troubling due to fact, overwhelming majority of startup leaders, founders and very early-stage investors alike, fail to realize or accept most corporations and private equity funds make acquisitions based on strength of the leadership team far more than on technology, service, product or market. That is, the acquiring company is "purchasing" the strong leadership of the startup far more than the assets, products/services or markets of the startup, with intent to have these strong leaders develop teams within the acquiring company. While creating an issue with early-stage deal flow here in the developed world. Impact of shortage of quality startup leadership, of leaders, is far greater in emerging markets and substantially negative in developing markets.

Before investor fatigue set in, solution was volume, with early-stage investors constantly adding to their portfolios, walking away from any startup leadership team required more than minimal input. Relying on the numbers game. As result, despite many startups and startup leaders possessing real value given proper guidance and input, over 75% all investments fail, amounting to nearly $400 Billion in losses annually. This number is misleading however as direct dollar in to direct dollar not returned is not a proper calculation of overall loss.

Regardless whether self, crowd or investor backed, most startups fail due to poor execution, absence of a quality leader or simply failure to lead. In a 2012 article in Fast Company, Faisal Hoque, articulated the reason, with both investors and entrepreneurs at fault. This is due to Investors placing importance on financial valuation rather than operational capacity valuation. Relying on, "[t]he theory that in a numbers game, some will win and some will lose…" which he goes on to state, …"is not an acceptable approach…" At the same time, entrepreneurs generally lack an Operating Blueprint consisting of a 360^0 view of their enterprise with impact analysis established upon appropriate scenarios.

Starving for entrepreneurial and investor leadership. Patrick Henry in a 2018 Entrepreneur article, drawing upon his own experience as an entrepreneur and startup consultant and on industry research, lists a number of reasons why startups fail, while making the case each item is due to one single issue, "… each of these reasons for failure is due to a failure in leadership at some level." From direct experience with my own failed startups, as both entrepreneur and investor, I find Faisal Hoque's assessment to be spot on, however for the reason Patrick Henry states. We are lacking entrepreneurial and investor leadership, despite heavy investments in all the many entrepreneurial programs springing up around the world.

I find I must agree with my friends and colleagues in the investment community, many of whom have been investing for decades, leaders are harder to find. Over the years I've written about leadership, similarities between startup and Special Operations environments and requirements, on challenges and tools to develop leadership individually and within a startup team. During the course of twenty years in and around the technology startup industry and ten years in Special Forces, I've watched as the number of quality leaders, in virtually every industry and line of effort at all levels, has continued to decline. Despite herculean efforts and investments in leadership development programs, which are in truth, management development programs.

At very most basic, reason for scarcity is leaders can't be mass produced. Even more blunt, leaders can only be developed by already proven leaders. Which doesn't mean someone with more education, or money, a better network or a formal title and position with a prestigious entity. Rather, only by someone with proven experience solving real problems. As well, educational programs and professional consulting efforts conflating management with leadership, attempting to develop leaders using manager development tools, processes and resources fail at the task. Investor models, practices and limited investor interactions with founders are also utterly incapable. Even powerful Boards and seasoned advisors providing solid advice to founders on aspects of their business, are not the solution. Leaders must develop leaders and not in the classroom, but out there in the wild.

For startups on the verge of failure, failure to raise initial Capital or follow-on Capital, leadership is everything, both at level of entrepreneur and investor. Only solution for these failing startups, those with actual potential to realize returns, is at least one active investor who is also a proven leader. This is due to the truth, rapidly identifying and developing leadership while turning around a startup on the verge of failing is a nearly impossible task, requiring substantial time and effort from at least one highly experienced individual. Time and experience virtually all founders and most investors, board members and advisors simply don't have, the latter two mostly due to extensive depth of other obligations.

For failing startups, in rare cases where an active investor does have an interest to be more involved, five indicators must exist in the final decision maker "leader" of the startup, before the interested investor can entertain contributing more of their network, resources, Capital and incredibly limited time:

1- **Ability to see and listen –** Constantly learning from everything, at all times. Even when in heightened states of stress, such as when confronted with the very real possibility of failing – finding a way;

2- **Reality above all –** Where others retreat into comfortable illusions and provide a false front, leaders live in the very real world and find ways to bring others into that world – building consensus;

3- **Calm under fire –** While the internal self may be under extreme stress, facing doubt and concern, outwardly there is only calm resolve – putting mission first;

4- **Influence –** Understanding the team, influencing individuals to rise to their own leadership potential in their given domain, rather than dictating tasks to be accomplished and how – Influence-based leadership; and

Perhaps as much as fifty percent or more of failing startups could exit and realize real returns with right guidance for and leadership development of the founder, active, hands-on mentoring. Of the ninety-eight percent of startups don't receive even initial funding, perhaps as much as twenty percent of these could, matched with right active investor leadership and mentoring. Reason return numbers could increase by this much is due to latent leadership existing in great volumes, all around the world, to include in failing and failing to launch startups. To include within communities and among peoples never before imagined. The numbers game, heavy investments in all the many programs intended to foster entrepreneurship, and impact investing, are incapable of the active investor leadership required.

Identifying and developing leaders requires considerable, direct and personal hands on engagement from individuals who have found and proven their own leadership capacities. Twenty years ago, during NextCard days, two individuals in particular, Shaun Deane and John Rouleau, showed me the critical importance of the hands-on approach to leadership development. Not giving up, taking time out of their incredibly busy schedules to help me mold and shape my thinking, to overcome experience deficits and Irish pig-headed stubbornness. Very same issues most startup leaders and many early-stage investors face in themselves.

Now, with two decades of leadership behind me, one in Special Forces and one leading my own startups and investments, I've come to truly appreciate from experience, leadership is everywhere, solid leadership. There are real returns out there in startups all over the world, in developed, developing and emerging markets. Returns from modern securitized, knowledge economy startups which need not fail, or which should launch. However, at present most all is little more than potential, trillions of dollars of unrealized potential, untapped Alpha. Without more active investors, leaders, actively developing startup leaders and other investors, that is all it will remain. Unrealized potential. Of course, cadre of active early-stage investment leaders is the critical, often missing, component.

It's time for highly successful 'active' Angel, Seed and early-stage Venture investors to, as in Special Forces, train the trainer. If one hundred highly proven investors committed to training one investor from outside their circle, this hundred would train one hundred, that hundred would train…soon numbers early-stage investors around the world becomes a staggering number. Investors backing and developing startup leaders. Startup leaders creating opportunities, using technology and business to solve real problems, adding vast sums to global wealth. More important, generating demand for the increasing number of citizens around the world now educating themselves and seeking work close to home, to use hard earned and developed skills, to build their own fortunes, make their own contributions.

Fortunately, there exists a proven 'train the trainer' model for this broad-spectrum leadership development, a model used to great effect. US Army Special Forces, the Green Berets, possess more than seventy years' experience developing leaders, leaders to seek out and develop yet more leaders. Leaders to be found and developed in every corner of the world, under every imaginable condition from peace to war, and at every level, from the poorest, least educated individual in the street up through to the most educated heads of state in halls of power.

3 A GEEK GOES TO WAR

"In the startup world, you're either a genius or an idiot. You're never just an ordinary guy trying to get through the day."
– Marc Andreessen – Venture Capitalist

Native of N. Africa, you are recognized today as perhaps the greatest tactical strategist of all time. It's the Second Punic War, and you're Carthaginian general Hannibal Barca (247–182 BCE). Prior to invading the Roman Republic, you stated, "aut viam inveniam aut faciam – I will either find a way or make one" when asked how you would get your army, including men, supplies, equipment, elephants and weapons of war across the Alps. You're a gifted logistician, understanding armies move on their bellies. For fifteen years you'll live up to your claim, time and time again, finding a way or making one. With limited resources, always in enemy territory, you'll bring the Roman Republic to its knees, defeating her Legions again and again, often against all odds.

This wasn't enough however, being one of, if not the greatest tactical mind and, military leader of all time. In the end failure to understand your own Carthaginian people would be your demise. While you created the opportunity, Carthage failed to provide enough resources and manpower to go on and defeat Rome. Choosing to keep for herself. Instead giving you bare necessities, just enough for you to tie Rome's Legions up in Italy, using you as inconvenience rather than conqueror. Eventually, Rome used your playbook against you, drawing you to Carthage and defeating you at the Battle of Zama. Proving, genius, drive, leadership and loyalty of your army, experience and action are important. But active and fully committed support of other leaders is everything.

***

Late '08, my early forties, when I set on path to see if had what it took to become a Green Beret, never imagined skills and mind, developed as entrepreneur and investor would apply. At time, thought I'd have to learn entirely new set of skills, train myself to think in entirely new ways. A daunting task at any age, harder for someone my age. Old dog, new tricks stuff. One thing I was certain I'd to do, to improve my leadership capacities, was learning to be a team player. Not being a good team player was something recognized early in my life, being rather reclusive by nature.

It's why I never really played team sports, nor went to SF

Selection when a much younger man in the Army mid '80s through mid '90s. I knew however, if I was going to be truly successful, make a real impact kind, I was going to have to be a far better team player. No better way to learn than as GB on a team in the crucible of Special Forces at war. Much to my surprise, the world of Angel & Seed Investors, entrepreneurs and their startup tech companies and that of Green Berets and Special Forces proved to be quite similar. Both require selecting for and developing leaders, leaders who go on and develop other leaders. Both act as active and hands-on advisors and mentors out in the Last Mile, creating and growing assets together with local leaders, in environments of inordinately high degrees of Uncertainty and Risk.

In the high-paced and hyper-competitive world of startup investing, identifying, developing and hands-on mentoring startup leaders is everything for the Angel, Seed and even early-stage Venture Capital investor. Preventing wealth destruction and related loss of shareholder and stakeholder value and commitment requires strong leaders. Leaders capable of making solid decisions in times of prolonged high stress and limited information, capable of leading highly skilled and intelligent teams and team members along a sudden, dramatic pivot or pivots in the business model. In my first startup I was not yet a strong enough leader to influence my team along an all critical pivot nor to lead our investors to support us in that pivot. This lack of understanding what was required ultimately of me as a leader led to the failure of our startup.

In the high-paced and hyper-critical world of Special Forces, identifying, teaching, training, developing and hands-on advising leaders in countries and communities all over the world is everything for local, national, regional and even global peace and stability. Just as with the world of startups, though with the added burden of preventing loss of life, at least those of teammates, colleagues and innocents, in Special Forces, preventing asset destruction and related loss of shareholder and stakeholder value and commitment also requires strong leaders. Leaders capable of making solid decisions in times of prolonged incredibly high stress and limited information, capable of leading both skilled and unskilled, educated and uneducated teams and team members along a sudden, dramatic pivot or pivots in operational strategy.

During the year and a half of the Special Forces Qualification Course, after, while conducting Village Stability Operations in Afghanistan and after conducting counterterrorism and counter proliferation operations in Asia. Eight Truths about leaders distilled in my mind. Truths with a capital T. Because they seem to be hardwired into leaders, even leaders with only latent, little developed, leadership capacity. Skilled managers allude to these Truths, while leaders live them in all they do. These Truths, pervading throughout mission planning, preparation, execution and after-action review, are now integral to all I do as once again technology entrepreneur and investor and in all my entrepreneurial mentoring.

- **First Truth –** market research, always do your own detailed research, conduct your own Intelligence Preparation of the Battlefield. No matter how extensive intelligence collection and analysis are, all intelligence is outdated, incomplete and contextually irrelevant to your specific mission. Only you can truly know your enemy, your friendlies and the space and complex ways in which these two interact and how a change in any piece of information leads to movements to be benefitted from or defended against.

- **Second Truth –** business planning, conduct extensive planning before you ever initiate operations, as failure is not an option when real lives and real assets are at stake in an environment where things will go wrong, even catastrophically. Planning must consist of a detailed operational strategy denoting necessary and available resources and personnel, movements and activity over time, phases of operation with abort criteria, multiple courses of action, communication plans, Risk factors with mitigation strategies for each, and contingency planning providing for maximal Return on Investment in the event of predictable failures.

- **Third Truth –** team selection, your team is absolutely everything and group think kills. Ideas and plans are critical to success, but when first shot is fired, even the best plan is obviated. When this happens, and it always does, success is derived almost solely from having the right mix of personnel with the right combinations of continually improved hard and soft skills, individual leadership capacities and uniquely different personalities such that group think does not prevail and prevent success conducting ever changing contingency operations, pivots in the strategy.

- **Fourth Truth –** partnerships & alliances, it's impossible to possess enough resources, relationships and access to accomplish the mission alone. Even if partners or allies don't do it exactly as you, as good as you, or represent a cost you don't want to bear, have them involved from the start. The Network Effect is powerful. And no one is always right nor always successful. Only through investing heavily in and committing fully to the success of your partners and allies can your own success be realized when things are not going well.

- **Fifth Truth –** contingency planning, there are such things as no win situations, Kobayashi Maru level impossible situations will occur. In these times it's absolutely essential to maintain the calm necessary for rational and logical thought. Calm requires contemplation and planning, in particular, contingency planning. Most any situation, no matter how catastrophic, allows for a means to survive and even realize a return if calm minds exist and prevail against the chaos.

- **Sixth Truth –** brand recognition, those in direct line of fire, out in the front, taking fire and casualties are ones to receive greatest credit for the win. However, no one is ever alone in the line of fire, nor did they get there without support of their network, allies and partners. Always remain the Quiet Professional, not the silent professional, humble and giving to and sharing praise with all those who were involved in enabling you to attain the win.

- **Seventh Truth –** vision, retain tactical patience, remain calm and stay the course due to the fact largest and most sustainable returns take time to develop no matter how many resources are applied or how favorable the starting conditions. This is true in a battle and across a battle campaign. Believe in your plan, in your team and partners and allies and in your ability to address contingencies, to collectively adjust the plan on the fly and to continue on in the same direction no matter what. Everything changes, even the bad. Remain resolute and never stop moving towards sound of gunfire.

- **Most Critical Truth of all –** communication. Always communicate, constantly engage with team, partners, allies and any and all involved, those with resources and livelihoods on the line. Communicate, no matter how bad the news may be, so all may survive, recover as much as is possible so they may regroup and return to the fight. It's easy when things are going well, but when things get hard and losses are occurring, only those who know you give a damn about their losses and gains will go the extra distance necessary to snatch victory from defeat.

During my time with the Regiment, conducting VSO and related combat action in Afghanistan, failure to adhere to any one or more of these Truths resulted almost immediately in death and destruction, of teammates, partner forces, allies and innocents alike. This immediate and dramatic response to failure to adhere to these Truths, forever seared their importance into my mind, rewiring me permanently. One further Truth, one preceded all others, was burned into me during this time and under these circumstances.

I recognized it wasn't enough to have a single strong leader. Each of us had to lead in our own domain and across domains. Because real effort requires a team of leaders. Meaning, no individual is enough, no matter how good a leader they may be. No single individual is capable of such effort on their own regardless intelligence, drive and experience. Meaning, a leader relies on other leaders, not merely on good managers. Though good managers are also essential. No mission can succeed without support of solid managers, particularly, solid managers in the many supporting elements.

Very same is in startups, in SF, leadership is required and must be developed at every level and in every discipline the team is composed of. For small teams, every individual on your team must maintain a running understanding of the Eight Truths as relates to their current mission and purpose, in context of greater ecosystem and effort the team resides and operates within. This means leaders must develop other leaders, not simply from higher order leader down but at times from lower order, skills specific, leader up. On an SF team this is well understood, as even the lowest ranking member might be forced to take higher order or even ultimate leadership at any moment. Understanding this, Green Berets, to include those straight out of the schoolhouse, are trained and conditioned to lead a force of up to six hundred, should need arise.

4 STARTUP TEAM OF THE US MILITARY

"I like opportunities that are addressing markets so big that even the management team can't get in its way."
– Donald T. Valentine – Father of Silicon Valley

It's latter part of the Sengoku Jidai "Warring States Period" of Feudal Japan. You, an eight-year-old boy, son of low-ranking samurai, formal training is about to begin on Mount Kurama north of what is today Tokyo. By age twelve you're an expert warrior. At sixteen you participate in your first battle, a night raid on Udo Castle and by eighteen you're recognized as a full-fledged samurai. You're not only samurai, you're one of only a small number in history to also be a ninja. You're recognized as a great team leader and are the hereditary heir to the Iga Ninja clan. Your ancestors served the Ashikaga-shoguns, before serving the Matsudaira family, who have since become the Tokugawa.

In only fifty-five years of life, you'll win widespread acclaim. Being given the name Oni No Hanzō for your fearless actions, small team leadership and seemingly magical ability to operate undetected, to influence the enemy and battlefield and to win against far superior forces. You'll rescue Tokugawa daughters from Kaminogō Castle in 1562, lay siege to Kakegawa Castle in 1569 and fight in the battle of Anegawa in 1570. In 1572 you'll win great acclaim in the Battle of Mi katagahara counterattacking vastly superior Takeda forces at the Tenryū River with only thirty men. You'll fight the Nobunaga in the Tenshō Iga War, defending your ninja homeland, 1579 and 1581.

1582, following the treacherous death of Oda Nobunaga, with 200 of your Iga and 100 Koga Ninjas, you save the life of Tokugawa Ieyasu and family members, moving them 200 Km through enemy territory in 5 days. You'll go on to serve in many more battles and actions, being credited with almost single-handedly ensuring the Tokugawa-Shogunate through brilliant combination of leadership, ninja skills and practices, small unit tactics and guerrilla warfare. You're Hattori Hanzō (1542-1596), consistently ranked among top five warriors of all time and one of the most popularized warriors in all of human history.

***

'All in' teamwork, true suborning of "I" to "Team", is something most of us really don't understand, unless having been under such demanding circumstances as combat and being forced to function as an integrated whole, seeing immediately costs of not coming together and working as one. Athletes on elite teams understand better than most, but athletes don't pay for mistakes and failures in blood and lives, those of enemies, innocents, allies and friends. As member of the SF Regiment, I had not only to understand the value, importance and power of teamwork. I also had to admit and accept being part of a team and teamwork are not things come naturally to most. Fact also true for introverted, contemplative and internal types, which most highly-skilled and intelligent startup members and virtually all leaders are, even the charismatic ones wear an extravert façade to great effect. Difficulties equally true in communities, units and teams with no or poor leadership and corresponding lack of respect and trust. Conditions in many, if not most, parts of the world where SF operates, and in many if not most, failing startups.

Working with startups there's always a difficult balance to maintain, as investor, advisor and often Board member, between my experience and requirement to allow management team to make their own decisions. Including bad decisions. This due to two hard constraints. Availability of my time and effort for any single company in our portfolio and need to limit personal liability. Meaning, while I might be the more experienced at the table, often substantially so in very early-stage startups, there are critical decisions only the management team can make. Not to say management can't take advisement from those with more experience dealing with intangibles, team members, advisors, mentors and the Board. It does most certainly mean management has to make all non-Board level decisions themselves. Which can be highly disconcerting for investors, shareholders and stakeholders alike, as it greatly increases Risk our investment/commitment will not realize all-important Return on Investment "ROI".

The Special Forces, twelve-man, Operational Detachment Alpha "ODA", is the 'startup team' for the US military, tasked with living and operating out in the Last Mile, in environments of ultra-high Rish and Uncertainty, identifying and developing leaders and assets and constantly improving assets values. Though as part of a larger effort, these teams for the most part are self-contained autonomous elements capable of and frequently operating independently, making their own decisions, particularly when behind enemy lines or in denied or semi-permissive environments. While ODAs are highly diverse, with a broad spectrum of skills and experience internally, each team is also specialized in a core capability and mission type, with some teams, such as HALO, Dive or DA and S/O teams, uber-focused and highly-specialized.

When selecting an ODA to conduct a specific mission, many Known factors are taken into consideration, such as specialty of the team and composite of sub-specialties contained in unique background of each member, local language proficiency, team internal resource availability and other such factors. How many members of the team have worked together before and for how long, under what conditions and in what missions. The team's knowledge of the battlespace (market intelligence), direct experience in country and region (track record & brand recognition), as well as existing relationships with the Country Team and Host Nation partnered forces (access to customers, partners, allies, vendors…), are only a few of many additional Known and knowable considerations.

These are almost exact analogs for considerations we look at when deciding whether to assemble or invest in a startup team. Though with an ODA, unlike startup investing, there's at least also a well-documented track record, individually and as a team, as well as a great degree of due diligence on individuals with backgrounds vetted to Secret and Top-Secret. This is not to mention the informal due diligence network where in such a small community someone you know knows the individual you are looking at and will provide an honest opinion. With opinions not always flattering but generally far more honest and enlightening than formal due diligence. Some of this exists here in Silicon Valley, which on investor side is also a very small community. It's basis for why investors prefer to invest in a startup team where at least one founder has already been through due diligence and successfully raised money, whether for current project or previous, even if previous venture failed.

Just as with startups and determining to invest or not, selecting an ODA for a mission also must take into account many intangibles:

- personality of the team, and does this match with the partner force and Country Team and whomever may be in higher command, **know your customer**;

- operational tempo of the ODA, recent death of colleagues and friends, which exhaust and destroy families and individuals leading to troops not being in the fight emotionally or mentally, **management capacity**;

- whether the mission enhances the skills, capabilities and reputation of the team, company, battalion and higher leading to greater capacity, **valuation improvement**;

- does the mission address real or perceived needs, and who is determining that need and what is their intent, value proposition, and should the resources of the team itself, its equipment and supporting elements be applied elsewhere or in another fashion, **problem statement**.

Having taken everything Known or knowable and much of the Known Unknowns into account, command makes a decision to give a specific team or teams the mission. From this point forward, the Team or Teams are responsible for making decisions on their own. Excepting of course those decisions which only command or higher can make. Very similar to investors having gone through due diligence and having invested in a startup must let startup management make their own decisions, short of those must be made by the Board or which require outside approval. This requires an incredible degree of trust in team and startup leadership. For small teams, ODA and startup, operating independently, this trust must extend not only to leadership, but to all members of the team. Investor and command alike must trust the individuals on the team, can and will function together as an integrated and fully functional team, regardless circumstances they may find themselves in. Particularly as both WILL be in difficult situations, the very nature of startups and Special Operations.

While I'll leave details on teambuilding and teamwork to the next book, Being a Team Player, it's important to note here, discussing leaders and leadership, a number of methods SF uses to ensure it's always developing leaders and leadership in every single thing it does. As stated, learning to be a team player was not something came naturally to me, nor was the journey a pleasant one for myself and those around. Truthfully, I didn't understand fully until sometime after I'd left the team and gone on to pursue PhD studies. Having had time to reflect on how fostering individual leadership through teamwork was baked into every single interaction in SF. From Selection through Qualification, subsequent schools, while on an ODA and after.

Always assessed – We've a saying, "you're always being assessed." From moment you arrive at Camp Mackall for Selection to day you leave the Regiment, you're being assessed. There are always higher order roles need personnel and people change over time.

Senior & Junior – As teachers, much like Jedi and Sith, there's always a Master and Padawan. Regardless rank or position, there's a senior–junior pairing, with senior teaching, training and mentoring junior as replacement, to become senior as soon as is possible;

Team first – We've another saying, "you're not a Green Beret till you've spent at least three years on a team." While schoolhouse is exhaustive, it only prepares. No amount of schooling can compare to lessons hard learned while serving with 11 other A-type GBs on an ODA.

Who Knows, Leads – With staggering blend of primary and secondary skills each GB and the team must maintain, there's always a GB who's SME on a given skill or topic. When that skill or topic is center, that SME leads, even if happens to be junior-most team member.

S%$# in Hall – Almost every mission SF conducts is zero-fail, meaning anyone can't master assigned skills and tasks or can't operate as part of a team or be implicitly trusted, finds their gear in the hall. It's not enough to be proficient, you MUST foremost be a team player.

The tools and methods used by SF, particularly team leadership and senior team members, to mold groups of A-Types and an Alpha here and there into a highly functional team, are really rather simple, ingenious and powerful. It's astounding patience teammates, each a leader in their own right, extend to us less than good team players, how many opportunities to get it right are allowed. But make no mistake about it, everything is being assessed, and if you can't put the team first, even if never developing into a full-fledged team player, then your S%$# will most certainly be in the hall. The team comes first always, because the mission is zero-fail and not failing requires a truly integrated and highly-functional team in the environments and doing the work of an ODA. The very same is true of an early-stage startup team. Startups are a zero-fail mission. Only failure of a startup means loss of reputation, jobs, Capital and wealth destruction, not loss of life can and does follow ODA failure.

Learning to be a good team player was a very long and very, very painful process. Process required I also become a far better leader. Process would've been impossible were it not for a small handful of specific individuals, proven leaders, all younger than I, who each at different times and in their own ways, were hugely impactful on my development as leader, team player, Green Beret and truthfully, as a human being. Both personally and professionally, I benefitted greatly from Special Forces heavy emphasis on hands-on leadership development, not only leadership, but leadership in the context of a team, on SF's understanding and reliance on proven fact, Leaders alone develop Leaders.

Which isn't to say any leader can develop any other leader. Another hard truth SF understands quite well. Something startup founders assembling their team, seeking advisors, mentors, board members and investors, and early-stage venture investors themselves, would do well to understand and accept. Choose carefully. More often than not, in many of the early-stage investments I've seen fail, it was the team failing to come together around the founder or co-founder. Also more often than not, this was due to misalignment between founder or co-founder and their advisors, mentors, board and investors. When seeking leaders to help you develop your own leadership, ensure there is common purpose and real synergies between you first. The most successful startup founders and investors do this before digging into particulars of the product or service and startup itself.

Another important factor, was that in truth, while I needed the hardships of team life and mentoring from recognized leaders, I learned to be a part of a team because I wanted to. No one learns to be a better leader and team player without intentionally seeking just that exact thing. No amount of training, tools or resources, no amount of organizational structure, no matter how many quality leaders you have about you. If you don't want to become a leader and team player, you won't. For me I recognized I had to, that being a team player was critical missing component in my arsenal of skills. I'd watched too many good startups with real market potential fail because leadership failed to bring the team together. In fact, most all failures were due to this.

There was another reason I wanted to learn to be a better leader and team player however, in particular, a good Green Beret. That had to do with the mission of Special Forces, Irregular Warfare. I was very interested to better understand the submission Unconventional Warfare and even more precisely, the D.I.M.E. mission[i] of Special Forces. The Diplomatic, Information, Military and Economic mission. The type of understanding can't be derived from Google searches, books and manuals but only from direct, hands-on experience. And that required I become a better leader and a team player, a tested, vetted and trusted member of a team. If I hoped to learn the advanced skills of IW and UW, of the DIME mission, and bring those skills and knowledge back to startups and startup investing, I was first going to have to earn my Green Beret. For me, there was only one way. The hard way evidently.

5 ENTREPRENEURSHIP IS UNCONVENTIONAL WARFARE

"Once you discover one simple fact, and that is everything around you that you call life, was made up by people that were no smarter than you."

– Steve Jobs – Co-Founder Apple

It's Eastern Zhou Period, Sixth Century BCE, and you're general, military strategist, writer and philosopher. Recognizing combat will always be required, you articulate however, use of force comes with great risks, limitations and costs. Particularly, bankruptcy and civil and social disintegration if conducted by a weak State. Which Chinese states are, in your time. Instead you recommend force be preserved as a precious resource not to be squandered, to be used only when decisive impact is assured. Unlike traditional military theorist, you do not lead with force, believing instead victory and defeat are psychological states. This requires instead of material and physical destruction, the forcing of enemy leaders and societies from a state of harmony to one of chaos, allowing for defeat first from within your enemy's own mind. A student of the Tao, you believe in transformations, in recognizable contours in such things as weather, terrain and even psychological states, the interplay between regular "cheng" and irregular "chi" forces. For you, warfare is a forcing of the enemy from one state to another along a contour of your choosing, a forcing accomplished with the very least expenditure and with the greatest impact as is possible, regardless means or method required.

Your way of war is Total War, with far greater part far from the battlefield of combat, relying heavily on deception, superior intelligence, knowing your enemy and their state of mind, on unconventional methods and means. You condemn any action undermines your own society, such as attrition of men, weapons and equipment in combat or in siege of well-fortified positions and cities. Total War developed and promoted by you favors attacking enemy morale, splitting alliances, evading battles, attacking by surprise, and more psychological attacks, like setting fires and employing terror weapons, such as poisoning wells and springs with the decaying bodies of your enemies. Your philosophy of attacking the enemy's strategy, yielding victory without combat, will go on to become perhaps the most widely employed theory ever, used for the next two thousand years around the world in conduct of general warfare and guerrilla warfare, diplomacy, business and many, many other domains. You're Sun Tzu (544-496 BCE), undisputed master and father of Unconventional Warfare.

***

Sweltering summer heat at the ultra-exclusive "John Wayne School for Wayward Boys," otherwise known as the Special Forces Qualification Course, or simply, the Q, Camp Mackall, North Carolina. Preparing and gearing up for Robin Sage, the Unconventional Warfare culmination exercise of the Q. Sitting through endless, barely survivable, PowerPoints on Intelligence Preparation of the Battlefield "IPB", the Military Decision-Making Process "MDMP" as applied by SF in conduct of Unconventional Warfare "UW" and many other presentations. Couldn't help putting all of it in context and connect to experience gained conducting startup "warfare". This is, I guess, because we can't help but process everything through many filters we develop in course of our personal and early professional lives, regardless what we may go on to do and accomplish after. Us engineers see things mechanistically. Soldiers see things militarily. Diplomats, geopolitically. And the list goes on and on. So, it shouldn't come as surprise I found correlations between Green Beret training and mission and my just previous life.

Part precocious mid-life crisis, part hit a wall in personal development needing to master teamwork, part something far bigger, brought me to this. Sitting with classmates. Soaking up mind-numbing classes before going into isolation planning for Robin Sage infill. Little more than a year earlier I'd meditated for eight months on where to apply myself next. That something far bigger proved to be solving Last Mile Problem of Finance. That is. Getting into world's poorest and most conflict-ridden and repressed communities, seeking out and developing local business leaders, repurposing local elites as modern investor class and investing together in securitized, knowledge economy startups.

Having firmly committed myself to this vision and purpose, 9/11 happened. Realized we didn't have time to enfranchise rest the world, modernize, through charity, aid and transfer payments nor through modern philanthropy now called Impact Investing. We needed to leapfrog these communities straight to globalization, much as mobile leapfrogged straight to mobile and mobile data without having to go through decades building out and supporting landline infrastructure business, investment and return models. This need to leapfrog local economies, and right now, was particularly true in increasing number of communities of the world riddled with conflict where aid, charity, transfer payments and impact investing can't reach even if they were the solution.

After spending seven years learning and gaining experience in Investment Banking and finance, Private Equity, Venture Capital and the securities markets and enhancing understanding of startups and startup life, in the US, EU and China. Turned my attention to getting into these conflict riddled communities, to what would take to make that possible. Realizing, if we were going to get into these communities, develop leaders, repurpose local elites, invest in startups, securitized assets, realize real rates of return. We were going to have to work with those with deep knowledge and experience, extensive relationships, in these very same communities. There was one organization in the world tasked with this type of thing, one community with body of practice and doctrine backed up with decades and decades of "ground truth" experience. That was the Green Berets of Special Forces specifically, but also the overall Special Operations community of the US Military and her allies and partners around the world. That SF was also world masters at developing leaders and team players, two skills I needed to also improve dramatically, was incredibly fortuitous. So, here I was, forty-three years old, soaking up doctrine and methodology in North Carolina. Trying hard not to fall asleep.

Before getting too deep in. For those not had opportunity to serve in SF or the military in general. Few definitions may be in order. For clarity,

Unconventional Warfare,

"…consists of activities conducted to enable a resistance movement or insurgency to coerce, disrupt or overthrow an occupying power or government by operating through or with an underground, auxiliary and guerrilla force in a denied area."

While the Military Decision-Making Process,

"…is a United States Army seven-step process for military decision making in both tactical and garrison environments."

And IPB is,

"…a systematic, continuous process of analyzing the threat and environment in a specific geographic area."

MDMP and IPB, as former startup guy, I understood quite well, without need of more tedious presentations. For our two startups I'd developed sixty plus page business plans with related twenty-five thousand interlocking cell financial spreadsheets. MDMP output at its finest. As to IPB. Had a decade experience with that. Both as entrepreneur conducting detailed research before writing business plans and later as analyst in Investment Banking, Private Equity and as associate in Venture Capital, skimming through or reviewing in detail fifty to a hundred business plans or more per month. In ten years, I'd reviewed literally thousands of IPB reports and the output of hundreds of MDMP sessions in form of market research reports and business plans and financials.

One thing I did pick up of great value from schoolhouses at Bragg and Mackall, beyond beginning understanding of real teamwork, was SF's streamlined, yet highly detailed formal process to get to a finished product. More I was exposed to a new format for finished product, the detailed 5 Paragraph Operations Order "OPORD"[ii] and the reduced and graphic oriented Concept of Operation "CONOP". Perhaps even more valuable, I was introduced to and became thoroughly familiar with how to break everything into component pieces and use the entire process from start to finish as a leadership and teambuilding exercise includes every individual on the team. Something we now require of all our startup teams and of ourselves.

This constant, detailed planning is what truly separates Green Berets of US Army Special Forces from all other Special Operations elements in the world. And it's how fully integrated and interwoven leadership and teamwork development is introduced early and then conducted throughout the Q. Even most junior Green Beret "Long Tabber" regardless age, former and current Military Occupational Specialty or any other consideration, is trained to develop a detailed map of the enemy and friendly situation along with of the physical battlefield. This knowledge is then used to drive highly detailed MDMP process leading to OPORD. In practice, the OPORD is broken into its many subsections and each member of the team is tasked with completing a portion, before reassembling, adding all together, developing proposed courses of action, wargaming these COAs and selecting COA with highest probability of success. This begins early in the Q. During Small Unit Tactics, every single candidate must demonstrate not only their ability to contribute to any given section of the OPORD, but to also, as leader, demonstrate ability to coordinate efforts among their team, culminating in final plan which is then executed in live simulation.

Reason each Green Beret must master intelligence development and planning, conduct constant IPB and MDMP, all while teaching leadership and teamwork, is at any moment, an ODA or any number of individuals from an ODA, to include a single GB, may be required to conduct any one or all of SF's Irregular Warfare missions anywhere in the world. Primary Irregular Warfare mission types SF conducts are: Unconventional Warfare; Foreign Internal Defense; Direct Action; Special Reconnaissance; Counter-Terrorism; Counter-Proliferation; Psychological Operations; and Information Operations. All require Green Berets, individually and collectively, regardless rank, position and time in service, on demand, to prove they can provide:

- **Highly detailed situational awareness –** know in depth your enemy, your friendlies, the movements within and across the battlespace, as well as available resources and allies, and most critically your team's abilities before ever taking on a task

- **Needs assessment –** early identify the many Risk and Uncertainty factors and constraints which limit your ability to succeed and identify necessary resources and milestones critical to success

- **Talent identification, development and leadership –** early recognize talent, foster and shape that talent through hands-on, active teaching, mentoring and leadership and enable that talent to go on to leadership, to train 100 others to the same level of proficiency

- **Execution and review –** develop self-sufficient and sustainable assets, maintain and apply these assets, all the while conducting after action reviews in order to make necessary corrections rapidly as dictated by current reality not preconceived notions, and most critical of all,

- **Successfully exit –** realize the required, or in catastrophic environments, the maximal possible, ROI and move immediately to planning for and conducting of follow-on operations, investments.

Even in today's "no business plan required" environment, some form of IPB and MDMP are required of a successful startup team and their early investors, and that represented in some form of definitive finished product. Even if only a CONOP, which is SpecOps equivalent of a startup Canvas. But more. Every real leader I've ever met, anywhere in the world, regardless industry or domain, regardless level of education or sophistication, keeps all of this in their head. Every single thing they do as a leader is according to the COA – Vision arises from this ongoing process and the constantly updated map they keep in their minds. Not to say that leader may not ask for inputs from team members or third-party experts, but not a one relies on these alone. SF teaches its members to collect their own information, conduct their own research, devise their own plans, and test these plans first. Even if later the GB finds they are supported with intelligence, logistics and other elements provide key components and functions.

Anyone's been an entrepreneur or investor in same will tell you these are exactly the skills and capacities required in startup environment, required of entrepreneur and their investor alike. Further, in startup world, much like world of Special Forces, all this must be accomplished with minimal personnel, time, resources or guidance, with minimal available information and often while greatly outnumbered and in a denied area, otherwise known as hostile territory, sic, startup marketplace. With 75% failure rates we have now, far too often, ability to do all of this is absent in startup teams and early-stage venture investors. Particularly those don't have least one startup success or failure behind them. In the Q, if a guy can't prove he can master this as leader of a team before finishing Robin Sage, he won't go on to wear the Green Beret and Long Tab.

Recommending the planning preparation and planning as well as individual and team leadership and teambuilding methods of SF as critical to startup founders, co-founders and their early venture investors is not a stretch. Most SF mission types and operational requirements can be mapped almost directly to those of the complex and rapidly changing startup environment. Some with little more than minor language, label and title changes. That the fast paced and uber-competitive world of startups is a battlespace, with Special

Operations like dynamics to be understood and mastered, is well-recognized. Many books have been written on the matter over the years. This emphasis on leader development and teambuilding, on intelligence gathering, analysis and planning by the GB is to ensure each can conduct the primary mission of SF, mission incredibly similar to the mission of startups. And that's Unconventional Warfare.

Best description of Unconventional Warfare was provided by President John F. Kennedy in a 1963 speech. "There is another type of warfare, new in its intensity, ancient in its origin. War by guerrillas, subversives, insurgents, assassins. War by ambush instead of by combat, by infiltration instead of aggression. Seeking victory by eroding and exhausting the enemy instead of engaging him. It preys on unrest."[iii] Conducted mostly covertly, UW is used to: overthrow an existing government or occupying power; disrupt operations of that power; and to coerce that power. Unlike conventional warfare reducing the enemy's military capacity directly using organic military forces, UW achieves victory indirectly, by-with-through proxy forces, employing subversion and guerilla warfare to reduce influence and credibility of the government with their people, causing the government to capitulate.

Green Berets, as ODAs, pairs, at times as individuals, insert deep behind enemy lines, train, equip and advise locals in opposition, developing and employing networks of guerilla fighters, auxiliaries and underground forces. This while spreading subversion and propaganda. Unlike CW which targets government and military power directly, UW targets psychology of civilian population, winning hearts and minds, at times using limited CW in surgical strikes to destroy military and government forces and facilities while leaving civilian infrastructure and populations relatively intact and untouched.

While in practice UW[iv] doesn't lend itself well to doctrine, to conventional systems and processes, things can then be managed. SF has developed quite the body of doctrine and practice around UW over the decades. Same is true with successful startups, with a considerable number of books written on the subject. In doctrine, UW is conducted in seven non-sequential phases. Although even in doctrine UW proves to not fit so easily into set patterns, as there's actually a very critical eighth phase. Which is tacked on uneasily using a zero. Rather than go all into mapping how UW and startups very similarly derive value from intangibles in environments of inordinately high Risk and Uncertainty. I'll instead only detail here types of Leaders and leadership required of each phase, in context of startups and startup investing. Starting with Phase-Zero.

- **Phase Zero – Steady State:** Your market/industry, without disruption. Where you develop general leadership, primarily through continued education and careful observation, while gaining experience and establishing relationships in the market/industry you work in and may one day intend to disrupt with a startup.

- **Phase One – Preparation:** You intend to disrupt a market/industry and now must prepare before launching your startup. Requires tailoring leadership, to unique culture of your market/industry, as well as to initial, co-founders, team you assemble. You must focus considerable amounts of specific study on every aspect of the market/industry you intend to disrupt, while establishing and developing far more targeted relationships and experience, all while refining your disruption, development and go to market strategies.

- **Phase Two – Initial Contact:** You're confident your disruption is possible, but you must assemble right co-founders, initial team, to include early-stage mentors and advisors as well as Angel/Seed investor/expert to test your concept in form of attaining requisite early funding. Now, mostly in stealth mode, you must ceaselessly refine leadership style/approach, market/industry research, and every aspect of your product/service, business, financial and operational strategy, assemble/grow your team, all while developing a minimum viable product or functioning prototype and preparing to go to market/seek additional funding.

- **Phase Three – Infiltration:** You continue to develop/iterate your product/service, team, approach. Proving all with early-stage investors, mentors, advisors, Board. Now you must think seriously about going to market. No one goes to market alone. You must carefully establish networks, with allies, vendors, partners, key hires. Must develop working relationships, revenue share models, pricing, distribution/delivery methods, positioning, brand development and marketing strategies. Now you're an organization, with expert co-founders, employees, overall team and network. You must improve and adapt your leadership to this new reality, beginning to focus more on leading a team to market than in product/service development.

- **Phase Four – Organization:** Your product/service is in testing, Beta, perhaps initial market penetration, steadily improving team and approach. Continually proving all with mentors, advisors, Board and follow-on investors. Focusing now firmly on market penetration you refine ally, vendor, partner, key hire strategies. Finalizing working relationships, revenue share models, pricing, distribution/delivery methods, positioning, brand development and marketing strategies. Your organization is growing, pursuing larger funding/financing, preparing for more rapid growth. Your leadership is evolving, preparing you as a brand, leading your organization and your network.

- **Phase Five – Build Up:** You, your team and network, now preparing for "game on". Still relatively low-key, you're aggressively building out, infrastructure, resources, personnel, funding and capitalization, networks and network capacity for sudden and rapid growth. You're expanding market penetration, conducting business on wider scope and scale, drawing attention of competitors and complementors alike. Now you, your team and network must begin to compete, requiring broader alliances and partnerships, brand recognition and greater market position defensibility. You're pursuing necessary larger funding/financing, strategic defensibility. You must think, act and lead strategically. Your leadership is changing yet again to that necessary of a rapidly growing and evolving organization and market. You now must include visionary, industry and market segment leadership.

- **Phase Six – Employment:** You, your team and network, running as hard and fast as they can. It's "game on". No longer low-key, you're ever more aggressively building out, infrastructure, resources, personnel, funding and capitalization, networks and network capacity scaling and trying to keep up with growth rate. Your expanding into new markets and market verticals, market penetration is expanding rapidly, as is competition and attacks, direct and indirect, requiring constant shifting and adjusting your business model and strategy, product/service mix and delivery and the team necessary for all. You're thinking, acting and leading strategically, without any respite. Yet again your leadership is changing. Now it's no longer enough to lead your organization, greater ecosystem, industry and market segment as brand and visionary. Now you must also be recognized as visionary across domains, in greater economic and social spheres as well. You're no longer leading only people and an organization, you're part of and leading portions of far greater, public and visible movement.

- **Phase Seven – Transition:** Yours is now firmly a corporation, widely recognized brand and market leader.

> While you're doing more than ever, in more markets and market verticals, rate of growth has slowed. You're increasingly stable and secure. Yet again you find you must adjust yourself and your organization and team. Your leadership. Now you must seek an exit, financial exit, in whole or in part, for you, your team, investors and all shareholders alike. This while protecting yourself and your corporation from all those you've done away with or displaced in the marketplace, your network and on your team, all the enemies you've inevitably created getting to this place. Your leadership has steadily adapted to that of leading senior executives and managers as your corporation is increasingly managed rather than led. It's now time to prepare your corporation for final transition to management, leading up to and post-exit.

There's no doctrine, no set pattern, system or process to develop this type of leadership or to follow this leadership evolution. Each must do it alone, in their own way, following the patterns of ebb and flow in their own organization and the greater ecosystem it belongs in. There are great books written by those who've done it, to act as rough guides, providing concepts and ideas as to leadership and its evolution you can adapt for yourself. From the world of UW and Special Forces, from my own experience in startups, I'll put forward the following.

1. Until you transition out from leading your startup, even should you be so fortunate to go on and develop it into a major corporation, you'll always be behind enemy lines, always under attack;

2. Your staunchest, most loyal followers, partners and allies will turn on you the instant they believe you don't share same interests and objectives, this requires Influence-based Leadership of a real Leader as it can't be maintained through force and bluster; and

3. Influence-based Leadership requires respect be earned, earned through proven proficiency in your domain and its

subtasks, more through seeking out and intentionally developing leaders, supporting the leadership of individuals on your team and among your partners and allies alike.

6 INFLUENCE-BASED LEADERSHIP

"When you were made a leader, you weren't given a crown, you were given the responsibility to bring out the best in others."

— Jack Welch – Former CEO GE

Despite being born to the Uriangkhai forest people, at 14 you follow your older brother's footsteps and join the Mongol horde. You're appointed by Genghis Khan as his door warden, allowing you to listen and learn. By age of 22 you demonstrate and prove you're driven by an Unconventional Warfare mind and by 24 you'll not only be a general, but one of the Khan's most trusted, feared and respected "Dogs of War". In a career spanning 59 years, you'll serve three Khans, directing more than 20 campaigns, conquering thirty-two nations, winning 65-five pitched battles, and conquering more territory than any other general in all human history. Having defeated the Hungarians, Georgians and Poles, having successfully invaded Kievan Rus, where it not for death of Ögedei Khan and return to Mongolia to select a successor, you would have gone on to conquered all of Europe, creating an empire spanning from the Pacific to the Atlantic across two continents.

Your victories resulted from unflinching acceptance of reality, reliance on unfettered imagination, quality intelligence gathering, sophisticated planning and particularly from your ability to lead, to coordinate efforts and movements, often commanding several armies in simultaneous battles separated by vast distances. It would not be till advent of radio and modern warfare in WWII, 700 years after your death, that battle plans and operations will reach your level of complexity and organization. Today you're recognized as perhaps the greatest leader of all time. Yours were armies based on meritocracy, employing and promoting to positions of high rank, even peasants and those from conquered lands and peoples, anyone proving their superior skills and capacities. At 73, still leading armies for your Khan, you'll die in China fighting the Song Dynasty. You're the undisputed Unconventional Warfare master, Sübügätäi (1175–1248) and there's never been your equal before or after.

***

Mostly in the West and Far East, since end WWI, dramatically since WWII, increasing even more dramatically during the Vietnam War and after, understanding for and acceptance of leadership role of the "Alpha" has been mostly, intentionally, lost. After two catastrophic world wars, with tens of millions killed, the Cold War with hundreds of millions killed, vast resources destroyed, it's only natural nature and role of Alphas would be questioned. It was not Alphas however who led the world to war, nor who drove such destruction and devastation, but rather it was aggressive A-Types employing force and the passive-aggressive types intentionally introducing destabilization. There is at same time no reducing fact was lack of strong Alpha Leadership, Influence-based Leadership, allowed it all to happen. While not the instigators, Alphas do still wear blame.

Starting mid part of last century, accelerating to this day. Rather than question value and role of the Alpha in order to improve Alphas and Alpha leadership. A concerted effort began and continues, with almost sole purpose of discrediting Alphas. Price for this removal of Alpha Leadership can be seen everywhere today, with increasing breakdown in the rule of law, rise of criminal, political and religious ideology-based insurgencies, and conflicts between nation states and between ethnic groups rising dramatically. Despite successful efforts to discredit, malign and mostly remove Alpha's and Alpha Influence-based Leadership from 'polite' civilization over last century plus, as professional managers and technocrats have taken on ever greater roles and responsibilities. As of this writing, all but 10 of 195 nations are not in some form of open conflict or outright war.

With this level of conflict, never experienced before in human history, not even at heights of WWII and the Cold War, it's increasingly difficult to argue removal of Alphas and their Influence-based Leadership is not leading to ever less civilized behaviour. With many parts of the world and an increasing number of communities realizing a very marked decline, regression, towards an earlier, more primitive, violent and totalitarian condition. As with most things in the age of Political Correctness, at heart of the problem is a failure in definition. Where Alphas, strong centered individuals acting as stabilizing influence in their group or community are now conflated with the aggressive, self-aggrandizing A-Type or as destabilizing passive-aggressive.

To be certain, in all of us there are competing interests and needs, which ebb and flow across every moment and stage of our lives, at times dramatically, pulling us in competing directions, destabilizing us. This is true at level of the individual, small teams, large groups, departments and organizations, societies, tribes, nations and across entire civilizations. This instability permeates through every single thing we do, say and create. In each of us some degree of instability exists at any given point in time and across all history, past, present and future. It's only nature being nature, primates being primates. True even with the very best, healthy environment and nurture. Without a powerful central core, requiring careful and diligent effort to develop over long periods of time.

Without sitting firmly in the Middle Way between competing interests and needs within ourselves as individuals and collectives. No matter systems and processes, regulations and laws and societal norms, punishments, developed, there will be instability. Instability preventing, creating illusion of or only allowing fleeting success at best. Or worse still, and far more prevalent, success only achievable at expense of others. This level of instability within each of us, becomes vastly more powerful when in groups, due to instability within each, compounded by that injected from A-Types, the passive-aggressive or simply through carelessness and inattention, is multiplied by total number of individuals. Without strong Alpha Leadership within ourselves, or at least within our group, society and civilization alike, instability multiplies out of control rapidly until there's only instability, chaos and conflict.

Being that strong central core, is the role of the Alpha, the centered individual, the immovable object against which unstoppable forces break themselves. Alphas are those who deconflict competing interests, ensuring stability is possible. This isn't to be confused with the counselors of many kinds who act as intermediaries. Alphas are Leaders – even when not the boss. The Alpha is one who remains resolutely focused on mission success alone, regardless competing forces within self, team or organization. The Alpha is one with strong inner discipline who uses influence rather than force, calm rather than chaos, constantly seeking stability, careful to not project their own inner world onto others. And in those rare instances where aggression and force are necessary. The Alpha ensures they are applied in incredibly precise measure and only exactly where and when needed, surgically.

This is not the descriptor used when defining an Alpha in our modern, Politically Correct, world, where individual strength and power is intentionally mislabeled and much maligned. We live in a time where we are told consensus, everyone being heard, is everything. And there is very real merit to this. However, consensus is impossible without strong figures, Alphas and their Influence-based Leadership. Without Alpha strength, acting as calm, rational counter, only voices heard, are those loudest and most demanding. Today, at time when chaos and tumult are rising, when we need them the most. Alphas have been relegated to the realm of history, relics, individuals not only no longer necessary, but something to be feared, marginalized and reduced to ineffectiveness. In my own lifetime, Alphas have been forced to mask themselves, hide their leadership, dissemble and allow what should not be allowed, that or be maligned and isolated so the mob may be turned against.

Today the bluster, aggression, leading by force of A-Types and the intentional destabilization of the passive-aggressive are believed to be telltale signs of an Alpha. Which is furthest thing from truth. Alphas do employ such tactics and methods. However, when an Alpha employs, it's because exactly that and only that is necessary, almost always due to too many A-Types "in charge" and too much management by the passive-aggressive. That bluster, aggression, force, intentional destabilization, self-orientation, are signs of an Alpha is a falsehood created by A-Types and the passive-aggressive to justify or mask their own failings and actions, their lack of talent or failure to develop existing talent. The Alpha on the other hand is one who, centered immovably in middle of their own path, ceaselessly and at times ruthlessly, improves self, moving fluidly within the Ikigai[v] Model. Improving self while tirelessly influencing others to develop themselves.

While true, A-Types and the passive-aggressive have set upon an effective campaign to malign Alphas, such is nature and the struggle between will always be. Why anti-Alpha sentiment has become the norm however has less to do with intentional efforts to malign, and instead has more to do with the age of management we've experienced this past one hundred plus years. As we've poured increasing effort into producing ever better managers, question has become one of if Alphas "Leaders" are necessary. Our incredibly skilled and educated managers got it. Right? Are not the technocrats the leaders we require now? Not so fast. Problem for management is complexity of today's world and the accelerating pace at which change is occurring. Despite incredible quality of modern management practices in era of highly refined specialists, despite growing numbers and power of technocrats, highly-capable generalists are still required. Look no further than GE and its demise post Jack Welch, despite having quite literally the world's foremost technocrats, managers and management development programs.

In times of sudden and rapid change, while quality management is essential, quality Leaders, Alphas and their all-important Influence-based Leadership, are absolutely critical. Someone has to lead, to have confidence necessary to get out there, take the big risks, be strong central figure, the one resolute and stable despite all the inevitable chaos and uncertainty of change. Someone has to provide a clear vision for the future, a vision management will employ their highly developed management skills to attain. Elon Musk and Richard Bronson, to name only two are perfect example of this type of Alpha Leadership, influencing rather than forcing, as pace of change is accelerating. Let's make no mistake, an Alpha "Leader" is a highly skilled generalist, some within a single broader domain, fewer across several domains and infinitesimally small number across many domains.

In an age of accelerating change, of ever greater degrees of complexity in all fields of endeavour, where highly refined specialization and well-tuned and highly detailed systems and processes are the norm. Being a truly well-rounded and skilled generalist, to level necessary to truly lead and not merely manage well. Requires years and decades even of self-sacrifice and disciplined knowledge, skill and experience attainment, testing and growth. This is what is meant by the Q and first three years on an ODA only prepare one to practice UW, UW and startup practice alike requiring incredibly well-rounded, broadly-rounded generalist Leaders and Influence-based Leadership. That's because, it's only the greatly experienced generalist, thoroughly versed in existing systems and processes, can step outside and look across systems and processes, perfected management structures, and see how to break these down, where to improve, augment, reassemble in order to ensure mission success.

In the worlds of startups and UW alike, it's not enough to have this deep knowledge and experience and resultant confidence. Confidence to look across systems, find new ways. There are academics and consultants, experts and individuals of many kinds, with this capacity. No, you must also lead and not by force or control, but through influence. In order to lead through influence, you must possess and demonstrate knowledge and experience in virtually every role and responsibility in your organization. Such, you can provide specific guidance to those many who cannot see the vision in its fullness. Specific guidance they require before they can apply themselves to realizing that vision, using the systems of management they've worked so hard to master.

In both startups and UW, we hire/attach experts who know their skills far better than we ever will. Proven professionals always in high demand. Individuals taking on opportunities, not looking for a better manager, but seeking to contribute to something real, to be led by a true visionary. Leading such individuals requires Influence-based Leadership. Period! And not the artificial "influence" of title or rank and position. But the earned influence of an Alpha. Of the individual Leader dedicates precious time and energy to finding individualized ways to influence others to not only employ previously hard-earned skills in new ways, but to push beyond and develop those skills and capacities in ways never before imagined.

It's just this, influence rather than control and domination, distinguishes the Alpha from A-Types and the passive-aggressive. Where former uses skill and experience, thorough understanding of individuals, factors and dynamics at play, willingness to create new processes and systems, to building consensus and ensure steady movement to eventual success. The latter use bluster and force, rank, titles, position, cult of personality, adherence to existing structures and processes and destabilization to attain control through force. Where the former is an Alpha, the Leader, no matter place in organizational hierarchy whether directly recognized as such or not. The later, those more than mere nuisance, are little more than a tyrant seeking titles and recognition, forcing their will on others, controlling. Leaders lead through influence. More precisely, they build up leadership in all those around them, providing a clear vision allows stable new systems and processes to emerge which ensure success, particularly in times of great and sudden change.

Alphas perpetually hone and refine their knowledge and experience in order to ensure higher and higher orders of contribution and stability are obtained. The A-Type and the passive-aggressive seek for nothing more than success in accomplishing the next objective, more often than not only benefitting themselves, caring nothing for stability or anything beyond the next target. The Alpha constantly monitors the dynamics within the team and organization, as well as looking to external threats, and employs influence in whatever form is necessary, to include at times aggression, force, violence and even chaos, but only with absolute surgical precision. This last, with sole purpose to ensure individuals, the team, the organization as a whole, go on to realize the mission, leaving behind improved assets before moving on prepared for the next task or mission.

While modern management is truly an incredible invention, addressing a staggering number of needs, and will always be absolutely necessary. Right now we need Leaders. The world needs Alphas now more than ever. The world needs individuals with capacity or believing they have capacity to be an Alpha, out there developing requisite confidence and calm through dedication and discipline over substantially protracted periods of time. These types of individuals need to step up and get to work leading in far greater numbers. Even if means you take hits from A-Types and the passive-aggressive. Those of you who've already developed the necessary skills, knowledge and experience, broad generalist skillset. You need to step forward and lead, quietly and respectfully, but openly. And those of you already leading, you need to pass down your skills, bring up the leader(s) to replace you, while moving on to lead larger teams and organizations to their own individual and group success.

This is true in all domains, academia, science, business, government, military and law enforcement, the arts and entertainment, and all other domains which make up the human world. More, teams and organizations need to actively seek out these Alphas in their midst. Don't be concerned by the quiet, calm and assured strength of a true Alpha. Rather than marginalizing and reducing them, welcome them, enfold and fully embrace this rare but so very critical capacity and type of individual. Because the only thing matters to them is your individual and collective development and success. You'll be astounded the burdens they already carry to move humanity or their subset of it forward. Don't be put off either if you yourself can't carry that level of burden or obligation. No Alpha would ever demand anyone to carry a load they are not capable of, and would instead, having taken time to understand you, find ways to influence you such that you improve yourself to whatever level you're capable of.

This isn't for everyone, this life of the Alpha, of leading through influence. Not all of us are cut out be Influence-based Leaders. Though having seen it myself all over the world, under virtually all types of circumstances. I believe most all of us have at least some capacity to be an Alpha, or more precisely, to have some Alpha tendencies allowing for at least some degree of Influence-based Leadership in our family, community or organization. I've also seen quite a number of individuals without this capacity go on to become good or even great managers, to lead as highly qualified, skilled and proven managers. Even this is not for everyone. Both required incredible commitments of time and effort to develop. If you think being and Alpha, leading through influence, having hard-earned that influence, is for you. Question becomes one of, so how does one develop themselves into an Alpha, an Influence-based Leader? To this question, there's only one simple, yet utterly difficult answer. Stop trying to be an Alpha or leader at all. Focus instead on mastering the art of being a student.

7 ACCIDENTAL LEADERSHIP

"The ability to learn is the most important quality a leader can have."

– Sheryl Sandberg – Technology Executive

You're a young French peasant girl. The year is 1412 and you've just been born to a poor tenant farming family in Domrémy, France. Like so many other young girls your age, you're raised to help around the farm, tend the animals and above all to be humble and pious. Much like all other girls your age, with very little to no opportunity to one day lead anything. No reason to think about or develop leadership skills. Though in time you do go on to be recognized as a respected animal handler and seamstress, a good manager of resources.

Then an event occurs in your life and suddenly you are thrust on the European stage, right into fire of the 100-year war. At age of seventeen you're given a suit of armour and a horse by the king of France, so you may accompany the French Army to Orléans which is under an English siege. At age of 18, between May 4th and May 7th, 1429, in a series of battles, you, leading from the front, the fortifications are taken. By June, after recovering from battle wounds and returning to the front once more, the English are routed. And despite all odds, against every expectation, this simple, poor farm girl, though her life was tragically cut short, proves to be one of the greatest and most widely recognized leaders in Western history, you are Joan d'Arc (1412 – 1431) the Patron Saint of France.

***

In Far East, there's an ancient concept, "Student becomes master, Master becomes student – 學生成為碩士，碩士成為學生." Some point, early on, as child studying Isshin-ryū Karate, my instructor said this to one of the older students. I was too young to understand, thinking, "yeah, yeah, yet another cool, undecipherable, statement." But it stuck with me. Despite diligently studying martial arts from China, Japan, Korea and Thailand under different masters more than 30 years. More than 40 years practicing Zen Buddhism, meditating, studying Asian philosophy, history and culture. Picking up several Asian languages along the way. Living and working in Japan and China, having traveled extensively throughout much of Asia. I still failed to understand.

In the West, we're taught ultimate goal of virtually everything we do is to move up the ranks, to one day become the Leader. We are indoctrinated with the belief we must dedicate ourselves wholly to our pursuit or profession, over sufficient periods of time, to move up through all rank and file until we've attained rank of leader. At same time, we're taught many conflicting things about leadership. That it's an innate trait only some possess. It can be developed in anyone. There are many different forms of leadership. There are different leadership styles. List of ideas as to leadership goes on and on. Entire libraries could be filled with nothing more than books and articles dedicated to this one subject. Entire academic careers and programs of research and study, consultancies, have been built upon concept and practice of leadership. In Special Forces, as stated, belief is the GB's always learning leadership, with schoolhouse and years as a junior on an ODA and everything thereafter specifically tailored to set GB firmly on path to becoming a Leader.

This heavy emphasis on developing leaders in Special Forces is perfect example of the West's heavy emphasis on leadership. Leadership is the overtly stated aim of the entire military system, every branch, in all nations at every level. Every single aspect of everything in the military is supposed to be about identifying and developing leaders. Leadership being penultimate aim of any and all. Much like the martial arts, the military employs educational forms, rituals, ranks and titles, processes and doctrine developed over thousands of years of practice. All designed to provide student, enlisted and officer alike, a path to mastery, to senior leadership. Formal study and education steadily increasing in complexity and sophistication as service member attains higher and higher degrees of proficiency, higher levels of responsibility and authority, as the service member "masters" leadership. Or so prevailing wisdom goes.

Wasn't until a couple years ago, looking over the Mediterranean from a friend's balcony north of Beirut. There determining whether we should begin investing in startups across the Levant. Meditating on this and other concerns. That I started to put it all together. To finally understand what it means for student to become master, only to become a student again. I'd just turned fifty there in the Liban. For more than thirty of those fifty years I'd pursued mastery of several domains, seeking to be a leader of ever greater responsibility. I thought I had. And then, in this ancient, incredible part of the world, overlooking the Eastern Med, all of a sudden in a humbling moment, I realized I'd been wrong all this time. Neither mastery nor leadership were anything I thought they were. Little over thirty years pursuing a professional career, roughly twenty combined years in the military and seventeen years in startups as entrepreneur and then investor. In that blinding flash of awareness, I realized all that time, everything I thought I was striving for was not in fact what I sought.

Misunderstanding I'd operated under for nearly forty years came in two forms. First was a misunderstanding of mastery. I'd believed mastery was spending one's life in dedicated study and practice, memorizing all the forms in all their complexity and nuanced ways to fill my head with such depth of knowledge of the given domain as to know everything about it. Well, that was wrong. Second was misunderstanding of leadership. I'd believed leadership was successfully moving up through the ranks to the highest rank. At each rank proving I'd filled my head with all the many forms, practices and complexities required of that rank. At each successive rank rising above all others who didn't or couldn't achieve same proof of work. Also, quite wrong. There in ancient Lebanon. After decades of business and military service, striving always to reach higher rank. Patterning myself after what I thought true leaders looked and acted like. As I hit the half century mark of living. Epiphany! Management is not Leadership, Leaders are not Managers.

All those years I'd diligently sought to become a leader. I was quite unknowingly, instead following educational systems, professional processes and practices, carefully researched and proven patterns all designed to develop quality managers. Ultimate being technocrat. We'd been conflating management with leadership, managers with leaders steadily since near beginning of the Industrial revolution. Steadily reducing role and importance of Alphas and their Influence-based Leadership in direct inverse proportion the entire time. Conflation and reduction accelerated greatly post WWI and went into near light speed post-WWII and ever since. Turns out all those I'd looked to for example of Leader had in fact been highly skilled and qualified Managers, Technocrats. So, what does a leader and leadership look like then?

I'd looked in face of true masters and leaders across broad spectrum of domains, from martial arts and Buddhism, to the military, business and finance, the sciences and academia, the arts and many other domains. And quite literally, at every societal level and in every corner of the world. Without exception, not a one of these individuals was anything at all like I expected – none fit a norm – not once did they talk of doc trine or forms or rituals, processes, none used jargon or dropped names or relied on formal definitions, titles or positions. Not a one referred to themselves as master or leader. Some few had but most had never even gone or never finished higher education. Not a one looked, talked or acted anything like the highly experienced and polished professional I believed I was supposed to look and act like.

To be honest, these masters, Alphas, true leaders, were all a bit odd, as if they were something different, as if they moved to a rhythm humanity doesn't normally move to. They didn't fit look or paradigm of what I'd been taught leader and master should. Without exception, every single one spoke calmly, almost jokingly, from a far deeper place of knowing, a place well beyond the need for recognition or understanding, praise from others. Strangely, each spoke and led in a very similar fashion, by doing and showing rather than telling or instructing. While absolutely resolute and confident in their knowledge, they acted as if they were only just beginning their study, just beginning to understand their craft. Often asking more questions than offering guidance or direction. They were like children with a new toy. Like nothing more than a highly-curious student. None more so than my former Aikido Sensei, Kimbal Anderson of

Komyozan.

So, what does it mean for student to become master, to once more become student? How does the Q and three years on an ODA only prepare a Green Beret to become a student of Special Operations, more directly, Unconventional Warfare? Why is prevailing thought here in Silicon Valley that you are not a true entrepreneur or investor until your first major failure? What does any of that have to do with developing or becoming an Alpha and Influence-based leadership? Or is this just all a bunch of Far Eastern Mysticism derived nonsense? Some cleverly spun Yoda-like articulations.

Dōgen Zenji (**道元禅師**; 1200 – 1253), great Zen Master, once stated one seeks half their life to attain enlightenment, then spends second half trying to understand what the hell they saw in very brief window of perfect knowing. He didn't mean literally half one's life, more that, in moment of mastery, one is reborn to a new self, a child that must start learning all over again. Dōgen was right, regardless whether seeking enlightenment or something less auspicious and unattainable, such as mastery of a domain and recognized leadership. In the moment one attains actual mastery, true, deep understanding, they realize immediately there is still a vast degree yet to be known even just in that domain alone. Never mind in all the legion other domains. In more simple language. Attaining mastery of your domain is like climbing out of a steep valley between two mountains. Moment you struggle your way up and crest top of one of the mountains. All you find are more valleys and mountains, even larger, stretching into the seeable distance.

Any truly dedicated student, seeking mastery of a domain must sacrifice virtually all to study of their craft. This over very long periods of time. Solitary practice leads down many nuanced paths of research, study and thought necessary to deeply know a thing. If fortunate enough to have followed the wending path correctly, in an instant the student attains actual mastery of their craft. Understanding. Mastery. In exact same instant realizing they must now throw out all they knew. They've quite literally reached a higher degree of knowing. Literally a physical rewiring of the brain. As evidenced in brain scans conducted on Zen Masters and others. Having attained this new state of awareness, means the student must start anew. The Master of one mountain, must now take upon themselves tackling of the next and the next... Most of us will never attempt this journey or will get off at some point long before attaining sudden full awareness.

Most of us will do so because getting to top of the mountain is an individual pursuit and we're social animals. These long stretches of time, difficult and solitary journeys walked almost alone, are not for most of us. Those few who do take the journey, are the Alphas, recognized Leaders. Masters of their domain. More, it's this accepting and taking the journey, attaining sudden knowing, before continuing on to next sudden mountain range, is where influence the Alpha possesses is derived.

This takes us to leadership. Virtually always confused with good management. To use concepts from Special Forces Advanced Reconnaissance, Target Analysis, and Exploitation Techniques Course "SFARTAETC". Leadership is like shooting done right. Where sound of weapon firing comes as surprise to the shooter, having combined without conscious thought, incredible mix of exact right skills necessary to strike with exact surgical precision, before moving effortlessly on to next target. Zen and the Art of Archery type of stuff. This requires base and advanced skills mastered to such degree they no longer need be thought of. The shooter is now free to focus on higher level – battlespace as a whole – consciousness.

Moving effortlessly from target to target. Meaning, leadership is incidental, something arises naturally from your emphasis on getting basic and advanced skills and their combinations right. In simplest terms, recognition as a leader should be accidental and incidental to lifelong pursuit of becoming a Master of your domain. Something just arises when you're so diligently dedicated to reaching and are so actively moving towards that next mountain top, you look behind and around you to find others following you and it surprises you.

If you want to develop into an Alpha or to develop Alpha-like capacities, to exercise Influence-based Leadership. You must seek mastery of a domain, doesn't matter what it is, entrepreneur, investor, Green beret, painter, clown, anything really. Commit to moving beyond being simply a perpetual student. Someone tinkers with honing a craft but never fully commits to the solitary journey required of mastery. Set a clearly defined, comprehensive and highly difficult to obtain objective and accomplish it fully. Master it. As example, go to Special Forces Assessment and Selection, get selected, finish the Special Forces Qualification Course and serve at least three years on an ODA. And when you've done this, understand and accept you've finally only obtained the rank of first degree master.

If you do all this or equivalent in your domain. With such achievement always, irrespective domain, accomplished alone by you. You'll find while you've accomplished a great deal more than most will attempt. You've only actually moved slightly beyond proficiency to proficiency and some initial understanding. 1st Dan – Shodan – 初段. First degree mastery. Where you'll be forced to accept, despite all time and all effort, this is only first stage of understanding. Only very first step towards becoming a true Master. Accept each successive higher level of mastery only makes one once more the student. As our TACs in the Q Course stated, obtaining that first degree of mastery, graduating the Q, and spending first three years on an ODA does nothing but prepare one to be an actual student, to begin the real lesson plan and learning found outside the schoolhouse in the real world. This is the path to Alpha, a Leader, to Influence-based Leadership. So get to it!

Should you look up and be surprised to find others following, during your 10,000 hours, your 5 years to first level mastery as discussed in my article published with LinkedIn, Special Forces, Entrepreneurship: Never Quit! Be like the Buddha, don't tell them what to do, give them tips and hints as to how they might pursue their own mastery. Share some of the knowledge you've gained along the way as to how you overcame the difficult parts stumbled upon along the way. Help them see the destination, their next level of mastery, with greater clarity. As leadership is nothing more than this, having walked the path and from this alone having developed a clear Vision others can see as a destination. Then helping them on their own path as student to that destination.

What about all those who don't care to take this solitary journey, who've no desire to be an Alpha, whatever their reasons? This mean they can't be leaders? Not at all. Anyone can develop leadership, not simply quality management, but real Alpha tendencies. To whatever degree possible or desired, we should all strive for this. We should all strive to lead, regardless where we may be on our own path, regardless our rank, title, position. As we've learned in Special Forces, in decades of clandestine and covert operations and open war. Leadership may suddenly be thrust upon any one of us, at any moment. Best we be prepared to lead.

Who knows? You might surprise yourself and discover you have more Alpha tendencies, more Influence-based Leadership in you than you thought. We've certainly seen that more than once in Special Forces as well!

8 LEAD FROM ANY POSITION

"It is time for a new generation of leadership, to cope with the new problems and new opportunities. For there is a new world to be won."

– President John F. Kennedy – 35th US President

Imagine you're a Staff Sergeant Green Beret with covert Military Assistance Command, Vietnam – Studies and Observations Group "MACV-SOG". In the 54 months you serve in Vietnam you'll be wounded 14 times, awarded 8 Purple Hearts, Four Bronze Stars, a Silver Star and the Distinguished Service Cross among many other awards. For your actions you receive a direct commission, promoted from Master Sergeant to First Lieutenant. In one thirteen-month period, you'll be recommended for the Congressional Medal of Honor three separate times for three separate actions. First two awards are downgraded due to covert nature of missions. 1968 you receive the Medal of Honor for third nomination. And by end of your 36-year career, you'll be most highly decorated soldier of the Vietnam War, most highly decorated MoH recipient and most highly decorated soldier on active duty. And yet as a Quiet Professional, virtually no one will ever know your name. You're Colonel Robert Howard (1939-2009).

Your Medal of Honor Citation will read…

> For conspicuous gallantry and intrepidity in action at the risk of his life above and beyond the call of duty. 1st Lt. Howard (then SFC .), distinguished himself while serving as platoon sergeant of an American-Vietnamese platoon which was on a mission to rescue a missing American soldier in enemy controlled territory in the Republic of Vietnam. The platoon had left its helicopter landing zone and was moving out on its mission when it was attacked by an estimated 2-company force. During the initial engagement, 1st Lt. Howard was wounded and his weapon destroyed by a grenade explosion. 1st Lt. Howard saw his platoon leader had been wounded seriously and was exposed to fire. Although unable to walk, and weaponless, 1st Lt. Howard unhesitatingly crawled through a hail of fire to retrieve his wounded leader. As 1st Lt. Howard was administering first aid and removing the officer's equipment, an enemy bullet struck 1 of the ammunition pouches on the lieutenant's belt, detonating several magazines of ammunition. 1st Lt. Howard momentarily sought cover and then realizing that he must rejoin the platoon, which had been disorganized by the

> enemy attack, he again began dragging the seriously wounded officer toward the platoon area. Through his outstanding example of indomitable courage and bravery, 1st Lt. Howard was able to rally the platoon into an organized defense force. With complete disregard for his safety, 1st Lt. Howard crawled from position to position, administering first aid to the wounded, giving encouragement to the defenders and directing their fire on the encircling enemy. For 31/2 hours 1st Lt. Howard's small force and supporting aircraft successfully repulsed enemy attacks and finally were in sufficient control to permit the landing of rescue helicopters. 1st Lt. Howard personally supervised the loading of his men and did not leave the bullet-swept landing zone until all were aboard safely. 1st Lt. Howard's gallantry in action, his complete devotion to the welfare of his men at the risk of his life were in keeping with the highest traditions of the military service and reflect great credit on himself, his unit, and the U.S. Army.

***

In my own life I've been fortunate enough to have participated in a great number of things across a great number of domains, to have attained knowledge across a very broad array of subjects and experiences. But I've never built a billion-dollar company nor been an executive in a major corporation. Never developed cure for a disease nor algorithm to solve some NP Hard problem nor been a great teacher. Never participated in any major pitched battles nor attained high military rank. Like all of us, there's a vast world of things I've not done or accomplished. There's a vast number of individuals who've done far more than I have in their domain. Individuals who've accomplished and been recognized for great deeds. Individuals who've developed and proven strong management and even true Alpha Leadership. I've had great fortune to know more than a few of these individuals however, to have worked beside a few, even more, to be called friend. From each I've learned as much as I can, absorbed everything, in event higher levels of leadership are ever asked of me certainly. But mostly to simply be a better leader at the levels I've already achieved in domains I'm involved in.

Back to startups and leadership. Purpose of this book. Really doesn't matter your role in a startup, even in a well-established startup, even a Unicorn, with multiple successful Capital raises, with formal roles, responsibilities and hierarchical structure. A startup well into transition to management. You can still lead. At NextCard, long time ago now. Our receptionist was the most knowledgeable individual in the company. She knew everyone, what everyone was working on and even had the 'dirt' if needed. Never a gossip or tattle, she would quietly and unobtrusively share just the right piece of that information with just the right person at just the right time when she could see a storm brewing. Sadly, I've lost her name over last eighteen years. But I've never forgotten the lesson she taught me. Lead from any position.

This leading from any position is the strength of SF ODA. In fact, outside the Team Room, it's often hard to not believe the Junior Bravo (Weapons Sergeant) or Senior Charlie (Engineering Sergeant) or any member of the ODA are not team leader or team sergeant. This is due to a unique aspect of Special Forces and successful Startups alike. Something mentioned earlier. And that is, whomever is the leading expert for any given effort, is the leader for that effort, with entire team following their instructions. Even more precisely, while the 18B is the Weapons Sergeant, when working on weapons and weapon systems, it's the 18B who leads. And yet, might be the 18D, Medical Sergeant, who's most qualified on the particular weapon system training on our preparing to employ. So, the 18D leads, training everyone else, including the 18B on that weapon system. The best startup teams do the very same, particularly the early-stage startup teams we work with an invest in.

It's this fluidity of leadership within an SF ODA makes it so successful across a broad spectrum of operations and operational environments and provides it the ability to rapidly shift and adjust to environmental changes. This is not to say there isn't a strict leadership structure, either in an ODA or a startup team, nor to say such isn't important. Someone still has to be the final voice in decision-making processes and legal matters. Someone still has to be the Leader and the Boss. Outside final decision-making and legal structures however, no one is an authority in a given skillset except the one who actually is. Rank and title don't change that. When this skillset is needed. If it's your skillset. You should be ready to lead that effort, to at very least provide real Influence-based Leadership to the effort.

This can be very difficult for a startup team to grasp, or fully embrace, often due to a dominate founder or two or three having been surrounded by strategic "high-skilled" hires, under which everyone else conducts day to day business. The problem arises mostly from many founders or key hires believing they've to be an authority on all things related to the venture, or for the highly skilled and experienced staff the end-all be-all authority for that subject. As with an ODA has a senior 18B, if junior 18D went to latest school, or is one with hands-on experience with a given weapon or weapon system, the team is lesser off and may be in real danger, if formal roles and titles are stuck to and the senior 18B conducts the class or prepares the weapon or weapon system themselves. In startups, biggest problem arises however, more often than not, from business school education and business practices which talk about horizontal organizations, but which seem to be incapable of understanding how a truly horizontal organization works. Particularly as a true horizontal structure reduces need for management and power of managers.

In the Age of Management, era of ever more powerful Technocrats, business schools, meeting demand of corporations, non-profits, world-organizations, governments, even academia itself, are pumping out vast numbers of individuals who only understand hierarchy. Those above managing those below requiring good management skills. And those below working for and being managed by those above, requiring good follower skills. While still an hierarchical institution, Special Forces teaches every single member to be prepared to step forward, to lead at any moment. Whether that is to lead the ODA in a specific effort, a related effort or a completely independent effort created by the junior team member on the fly to meet an imminent need. Over the course of the past 60+ years Special Forces has become very good at teaching even its most junior members to lead from any position. As with Colonel Howard, MSG Roy Benavidez and others, SF also benefits greatly from real-world situations where junior members were forced to step forward, be the Alpha and employ Influence-based Leadership under fire. Lessons learned from direct experience, startups would benefit from greatly. More pertinent of these lessons for startup teams, are:

Never be a Follower – Every team member, regardless rank or title, while respecting the authority of experienced skill within others and the organization, must never-the-less think for themselves at all times. This ability is selected for in the Special Forces Assessment and Selection process and refined through leadership training throughout the Special Forces Qualification Course and the many leadership and specialty schools and duty after.

Respect Your Own Authority – Each and every member of the team is there for a reason, is there because they possess a critical skillset necessary to collective success. And at times, this skillset coupled with unique experience may be the most important in the entire organization and the individual must be capable of recognizing this. Throughout the Q and years of service after, each member of the ODA is put in positions where they must lead, so they may understand their right to lead arises from their carefully pursued and developed authority in a critical skill or skillset and not from rank and title alone.

When the Leader, Lead – Everyone has their own leaderships style and techniques, their own ways of influence, which must be carefully crafted and developed over time, whether that means leading only in a limited fashion as fitting your role or ultimate leadership of the whole organization. More importantly, as any single Green Beret may be called upon to lead up to 600 others at any given moment in most any environment, the Q curriculum is designed in such a fashion as to force the individual to discover, develop and prove their ability and willingness to lead.

This might be well and good for Special Forces going through 18-28 months of training emphasizing leadership before joining an ODA and attending many leadership and specialty skill building courses after. The question becomes one of how to introduce into your own routine or to your startup team, when you or your team are already task saturated and pace of development and market penetration alone prevent taking time to conduct or attend training. In very simplest terms, as we do in SF, develop your leadership developing leadership in others.

Following are a few recommendations as to how to introduce this lead from any position mentality into your own practice or that of your startup team:

Mentor – Give even the lowest member of your team something they can lead. Something as simple as a temporary project, or some key aspect of development leading from the skillset they were hired for. Ensure it is recognized they are the leader in this effort, even among senior leadership, and help them identify and develop their personal leadership style.

Recognize – There is no greater motivation than to be recognized for successful leadership by your peers, superiors and the world at large. Applaud loudly and openly the leadership of a given line of effort or project, giving credit to the individual, the team and then the company and its senior leadership. If fail, applaud what parts they got right before giving them a new task with clear guidance, so they get right back at it.

Listen – Perhaps the single hardest truth for founding teams to accept is they are not always the expert in the room, and at any given moment, depending on the need, the most junior individual in the room may very well be the authority. As Steve Jobs stated, these individuals were hired for a reason, listen to every single member of your team, let these authorities tell you what you have to do in their domain, which is why you hired them in the first place.

Step Up – If you're in a lower role in the startup, volunteer to lead a project or some subset thereof. Don't wait for someone to extend a leadership opportunity to you, seek it out, even if you fail. We all fail at many things in life, bettering our leadership from each failure. Push yourself to higher and higher levels of leadership. Watch and learn from those solid leaders around you. Not all of whom may have a title or rank in your startup. Look for those mastering their craft, while steadily mastering your own.

Leading from any position is no easy task, whether on an ODA or as a member of a startup team, requiring carefully developed skills and confidences, honed only through actual time as a leader, with increasing levels of difficulty. Perhaps the single greatest value derived from the exceedingly difficult task of successfully concluding SFAS and SFQC and that initial three years on an ODA, is confidence instilled through leadership challenges each and every member of the Special Forces Regiment are forced to successfully navigate. Not to mention all the many challenges after, to include those zero-fail challenges of combat and non-combat related Special Operations.

Many can't adopt this lead from any position mind, hence ultra-high attrition rates during SFAS and subsequent SFQC. Some of us are quite content being highly-skilled at what we do and for being recognized for that alone. There's real value in this as well. World needs highly capable specialists and managers. Holds true for startup teams as well. Not everyone wants to lead but identifying those who wish to and can and developing this in them, will greatly enhance the likelihood of success for your startup or investment, while also greatly developing your own leadership.

***

ABOUT THE AUTHOR

E.M. Burlingame is Founder – Honos Foundation, fostering entrepreneurship and investing in conflict repressed communities and Founder – Emerio Group, a technology developer and early-stage investment firm. E.M. studied Strategic Studies and Defense Analysis with emphasis on Special Operations and economic development at Norwich and is now completing his Doctoral studies in Interdisciplinary Engineering, with an emphasis on Computational Engineering at UAB. He's served with both 1st and 20th Special Forces Groups and previously with The Old Guard – Honor Guard, among other military service.

www.emerio.com

---

[i] For better understanding of DIME, see Dr. Newton Howard's paper, Diplomatic, Information, Military and Economic power (DIME): An effects modeling system.

[ii] For understanding of the 5 Paragraph Operations Order as a business plan, see Michael Penney's: 5 Paragraph Business Plan: The Action Oriented Business Management Tool For Leaders

[iii] President JFK: Commencement Address at American University, Washington, D.C., June 10, 1963

[iv] Excellent quick read for startup leaders and early investors, Unconventional Warfare Pocket Guide

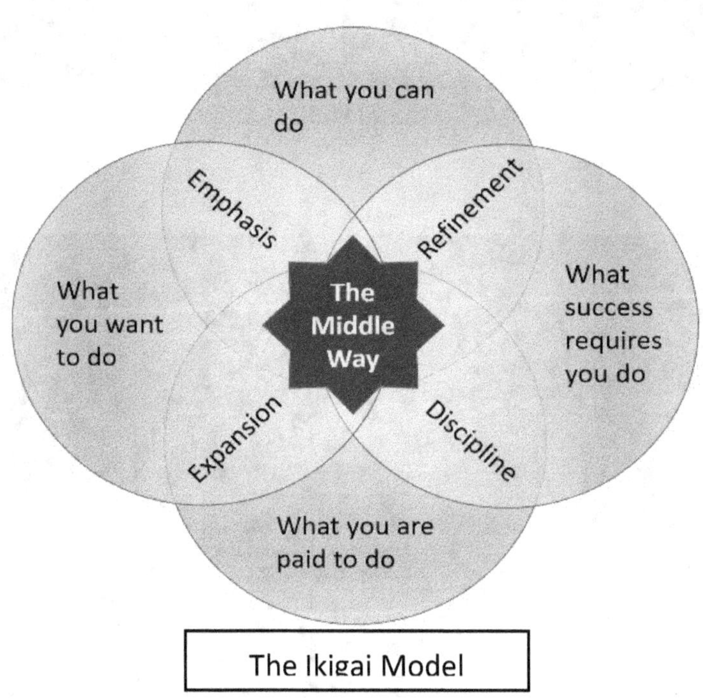

[v] The Ikigai Model

www.ingramcontent.com/pod-product-compliance
Lightning Source LLC
Chambersburg PA
CBHW071226220526
45468CB00002B/749

* 9 7 8 1 7 9 2 8 0 0 4 8 1 *